Silver Linings

Grandmother

Stories to Warm Your Heart

new seasons
TM

a division of Publications International, Ltd.

Contributing writers: Rebecca Christian, Gail Cohen, June Eaton, Glenda Emigh, Margaret Anne Huffman, Marie Jones, Donna Shryer, Nanette Thorsen-Snipes, Elizabeth Toole

Front cover: Christie's Images/SuperStock

Louis Weber, CEO
Publications International, Ltd.
7373 North Cicero Avenue
Lincolnwood, Illinois 60712

Permission is never granted for commercial purposes.

Manufactured in China.

8 7 6 5 4 3 2 1

ISBN: 0-7853-4470-5

Library of Congress Card Number: 00-110242

To _Marie_

From _Mary_

2006 - Cool Grandmothers together!

I carry Grandmother's gentle spirit with me,

like a lucky charm, or a special stone,

reminding me that I am always blessed

and forever loved wherever I may go.

Contents

A Trail of Flowers

Special relationships grow and bloom between grandchildren and their grandmothers. When a mother sees her children having children, her affections are compounded. Our grandmothers have loved us since the day we were born.

Grandmothers are blessed with breathing room. They don't have to go through the rigors of parenting again; discipline, responsibility, those inevitable hard times. Grandmothers provide welcome relief from the trials of growing up. They can even see themselves and their children mirrored in young eyes. And yes, grandmothers sometimes spoil their grandchildren—just a little.

This collection of stories celebrates the wonderful relationship that grandchildren have with their grandmothers. Some stories have been written by grandchildren. They loved their visits with Grandma. They shared their problems with her when there was nobody else that they could go to. After all, grandchildren appreciate the tender wisdom that only grandmas can give.

Other stories have been written through the wise, knowing eyes of grandmothers. These seasoned family members relish the exuberance of youth. They are invigorated by spending precious time with their grandchildren. Grandmothers have the pleasure of witnessing the development of the generations that follow them. The wisdom, understanding, and love that grandmas have to offer trickles down through the years, and sometimes travels many miles, to set seed in their grandchildren's hearts. They know that this seed will germinate and grow—a flower planted for the benefit of the future.

Enjoy these stories and keep them close to your heart. They are a trail of flowers, left for us and future generations to admire, contemplate, and delight in their fragrance. But most of all, they are here for us to love.

Grandmas Always Have Time

Sitting in my chair by the picture window in the living room, I can see the orange glow of the sun just creeping over the edge of Kangaroo Lake. The light filters through the leaves of the trees and sparkles in a dance on the motionless water. The faint sounds of sleep still linger in the house on this early summer morning.

This is my time. Just sitting and looking. Letting the restful silence creep into these old bones to rejuvenate me at the start of each new day. Soon the house will be rife with the unbridled energy and excitement of youth—always raised a notch when we're at the vacation house. But for now the sun is warming, and calm moments are strung effortlessly together.

"Mornin'," and I jump, startled to see my husband, Rob, at my side. "See any fish out there for me, Margie?"

"Scared me half out of my chair," I admonish. He bends to kiss my cheek, glancing my brow with his floppy fishing hat. "Coffee's on," I say as he makes his way to the kitchen. He's sneaking out for some early morning angling on the lake. Grandpa knows something about early morning silence, too.

I watch Rob step into the rowboat by the dock, scattering the glimmer of the sun in waves all around as the sounds of waking in the house are now stirring. My son, Tim, shuffles, sleepy and scratching, out of his room with his wife, Jill, in tow. *Guess it's time to get this crew going,* I think and shift to stand.

"Mornin' Mom," Tim says as he puts a hand on my shoulder as if to say "don't get up." "We'll get breakfast," he says with a yawn. "You sit and enjoy the lake. Dad out in the boat?" I just nod, knowing that the question is rhetorical.

Soon enough, rumpled heads of various sizes are darting this way and that. The older kids, always one step ahead of themselves, wolf down breakfast and head out to explore the woods around the lake.

"Hey Grandma," calls Steven as he follows Ann and her friend Casey out the door, "want to join us for a walk?"

"Sweet of you to ask, honey," although I know that his mother put him up to it, "but I think I'll sit this one out." He's off and down the steps in the blink of an eye.

"Can I come?" calls little Amanda from the breakfast table, holding a spoonful of hot cereal in midair. But Steven and the others are already gone.

Well, time to get a move on, I think as I head to the breakfast table to join Amanda, the youngest of my son's brood.

"Mom," says Tim as he sets a bowl of Cream of Wheat in front of me, "Jill and I are gonna head into town. Hold down the fort, OK?" He bends to kiss Amanda on the forehead and he's out the door, his Jeep crunching down the gravel drive in a cloud of dust.

"I wanna go to town too," says Amanda with a pout, looking down into her cereal with her bottom lip curled out. I can't help but smile. So precious. "I s'pose you're going, too," she says with a crack in her voice. She slips off her chair and starts to run off toward her room. But Grandma's too quick for that. With an easy sweep of my arm she's on my lap, her face still turned down.

"Honey, Grandma always has time for you." Our eyes meet and her frown turns around. Then I see that the sparkle from the lake hasn't disappeared into day, but is now living between our gaze. She throws her arms around my neck and I say, "Now that we are finally by ourselves, what shall we do today?"

Grandma is the sun, and the family orbits around her. She gives light and warmth, and she's present with us even when we can't see her.

The Berry Picker

*D*riving by the raspberry field today, I saw some children picking raspberries with their parents. It doesn't seem so long ago that I was among them. I remember a cool morning dew sopped my shoes to squishing as I walked with the rest of the pickers toward the raspberry fields. At ten years old, this was my first day of gainful employment. The thought of earning ten cents a quart propelled me on this auspicious outing. New school clothes, new books, or maybe, if I picked for a few days, a new radio—what more could a kid want?

As the day progressed, and the sun started to beat down on us, I longed for that wet morning chill. My throat was constantly parched. I never knew how good a swallow of tepid water from a tin cup could taste!

I knew I would see raspberries in my sleep that night. How could anything that left such a sticky mess on your fingers and briar-scratched arms taste so good? My favorite raspberry dessert was cobbler—warm from the oven with a scoop of melting vanilla ice cream. We seldom had it, though, because everyone else in my family preferred pie.

The day after my tiring tour of duty, I walked with my grandmother to her own berry patch. If there was anything in the world I was qualified to do, it was picking raspberries, so I started to help. She stopped me gently, spread out her quilt, and told me to sit in the shade. "You worked hard yesterday," she explained when I protested. "Today you rest."

On the walk home, I asked if she planned to make a pie with her newly picked fruit. "No," she said, smiling down at me, "I think it's time we had a cobbler."

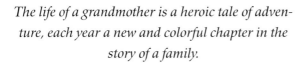

The life of a grandmother is a heroic tale of adventure, each year a new and colorful chapter in the story of a family.

New Lives

Going out for a long pass, I snatched the football from the crisp night air. Reception! Running backward, I tripped over the rake and fell, winded but triumphant, over the goal line.

The only player on my team looked down at me with concern. "Granny Ruth, are you okay?"

If anyone had told me two years ago at my retirement party that I would be interrupting my serious housecleaning for an impromptu football game on the front lawn at nine o'clock on a Saturday night, I would've peered over the top of my trifocals and muttered a serious "hruummph."

That was before Jeremy, my eight-year-old grandson, came to live with me a year ago last summer.

It was tragedy—a plane crash that took his mommy and daddy, my son—that brought Jeremy to my front door. It was duty that made me take him in. It was love, and then joy, that convinced me to let him stay. And, I'll always believe that it was football that really made him want to stay.

It could truly be said of me that I'd "been there, done that." Retired from a career in science and exploration as a photo journalist, I was ready to sit back and putter. I was relishing what I'd never had before: time for myself, by myself.

I'd raised three children, buried two husbands, excelled in my career, and served on more committees than my old dog has fleas. School plays, parent-teacher conferences, birthday parties, and skinned knees. I enjoyed my nine grandchildren when they came to visit or when I went to their houses; we were quite close. But I was always happy to get back to my own routine. In short, I'd earned every wrinkle, every gray hair, and, as I was fond of telling anyone and everyone, every precious, comfortable, free hour ahead of me.

Too much retirement, however, can make old ladies smashing bores. My daily routine was so clearly outlined that the excitement of unpredictability had vanished. Depression was peeking around the corner. A feeling of having outlived one's usefulness was starting to dominate too many conversations with old friends.

And then Jeremy came home with me after his parents' funeral. He was dazed, grief-stricken, totally at a loss: a mirror image of me.

Too much retirement, I quickly discovered, also makes Granny Ruth a dull playmate. Jeremy, who was restless with creative energy and trying to keep his mind off the accident, simply wouldn't stand for it.

He made games out of everything: cooking and eating pancake breakfasts outdoors; washing the dog (who, like me, discovered her second puppy-hood); and catching leaves falling from trees. He took me on hikes I thought I was too tired for; drew stories from my mind like water from a deep well; and coaxed me from the sidelines into enjoying games I thought I would detest.

I'm back in the classroom, the only white-haired homeroom-mother in the entire fourth grade. My aquarium is restocked, not with the fancy tropicals I've liked to collect, but with tadpoles and catfish. And, I must admit, I truly enjoyed playing Santa Claus again; and although Jeremy knows the truth, he humored me during the holidays. Christmas was a family Christmas again—for both of us.

People are always telling me that it's such a blessing that Jeremy has his old Granny Ruth. Nonsense. He's a blessing for me, changing my life in ways too marvelous to explain.

So I shouldn't have been surprised when I heard myself hollering to Jeremy, waist-deep in the leaves he was raking, "Heads up!" Without batting an eye, he dropped the rake and ran toward the "end zone" over by the walnut tree.

The ball, lifted by my toe, soared across the face of an orange harvest moon, gracefully cleared the telephone wires, and landed in Jeremy's outstretched arms. I can still kick a spectacular field goal.

And I'm sure that this would certainly have amused my son. I occasionally picture him sitting on the edge of a cloud looking down and cheering our gridiron plays. Sometimes it seems that I can smell his pipe smoke in the leaves that Jeremy and I burn. And one time Jeremy stopped, poised in midair, football in his arms, and looked over his shoulder as if he heard his father's "Go, go, go!" and his mother's "Be careful!" I try to say these things often enough for both of them.

Each night at bedtime, I collapse into my recliner and fire off a prayer that my knees will stay in working order and I'll have sense enough to follow where this beloved grandchild leads me, even if it is across a goal line dappled by the light of the moon.

Grandma's Favorite

$\mathcal{I}$ was in the kitchen chopping vegetables for supper one evening when I heard my daughters' voices drifting in from the family room. Our neighbor, a little girl named Nancy, was over. The girls were talking loudly as they played with their dolls. "Who is your grandma's favorite?" I heard Nancy ask.

"I am," all three of my daughters answered in unison.

"Come on! How could all of you be her favorite?" Nancy demanded.

"I know I'm her favorite because she takes me fishing," Debbie began. "She never takes you guys fishing!"

"Yeah, but that's because I can't stand to touch worms. Grandma takes me shopping," Janet put in. "And we always go out to lunch!"

"So what? That's because you like shopping. She'd take me shopping, too, if I liked it," Debbie protested.

Then Karen, my shy one, quietly asked, "What about the time I had chicken pox and I stayed at Grandma's house the whole time? She made me pudding or whatever I wanted every single day. I was sad when I got well."

I called my mother right away to tell her that if all three girls think they're her favorite, she must be doing something right!

When I was little, my family would visit Grandma. She would throw open her door and exclaim, "I'm so glad you're here!" Never again have I found such a welcoming threshold.

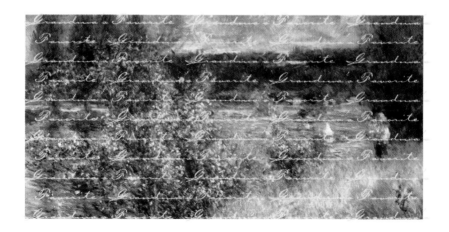

Keeping up With the Times

*I*n her drifting memories, the year is 1936. She knows that outside, passersby chitchat on cellular phones, minivans with airbags and built-in child safety seats ride the road, and hot temperatures produce nasty ozone warnings. The year is actually 2001, but in her mind, the music, the banter, and the dancing all hark back to a time more than six decades ago.

Estelle, at 80 years old, defies time, challenges old age, and only on very rare occasions succumbs to the subdued behavior expected of octogenarians. On this lovely afternoon, she feels particularly spry and pulls out her dusty, vinyl record collection. She has a yen to spin back to a different era and hum a tune from her past. The only problem, of course, is understanding how the family turntable works. The old record player has been replaced with a bank of electronics that looks like a command center for NASA—rectangular black boxes sprouting wires and flashing strobes of electric light.

"How do you work this thing," she yells to her grandson, Mike, as he blows through the room and bounds upstairs.

"Graaaaaaaaandma," Mike responds, with equal parts admonishment and amazement. "What are you doing playing around with that stuff? Where's Mom? What are you doing?"

"I want to listen to my records," replies the silver-haired woman.

Estelle has been living with her daughter and her family for about a year now, and, during that time, the grandchildren have come to tolerate the old woman and her whims. So, with no particular impatience, Mike pushes the appropriate buttons on the stereo, and electrified notes crackle to life.

"It's the 'King of Swing,' sweetie pie. That's Benny Goodman. How many hours did I listen to that man play his clarinet? Oh, my."

Holding her arms out, Estelle begins leading her surprised grandson through timeless steps around the living room. She explains that this is a wonderful dance called the "Big Apple."

"It's rather like a square dance, but with swing. Move your hips. Can't you move your hips?"

Estelle has lost a bit of her vigor but none of her moves. Paired with Mike's tentativeness, the speed of their impromptu dance is perfect. As the record spins, Estelle again transcends time and becomes a previous self, recalling thoughts from a long time ago. She regales her grandson with stories about Shirley Temple showing her adorable dimples; Greta Garbo arching her infamous eyebrows; Cary Grant winning every young girl's heart; and Franklin Delano Roosevelt capturing his second term handily. It was not an easy era, but it did have passion. Mike smiles as they dance.

After the Big Apple segues into the jitterbug and then into the Lindy hop, Mike mugs a mischievous grin—not unlike the smirk he wore when his grandma caught him smoking under her big, weather-beaten back porch steps.

"Now let me show you a few moves, Grandma." Always open to new ideas, Estelle watches as Mike replaces black vinyl with silvery plastic. The notes change from swing to pop; bass overpowers treble. "It's 98 Degrees, Grammy. They're really cool. Now, move your hips this way, Grammy. Let your arms go. Follow me. . . . "

"This is silly," Estelle giggles. "But my grandmother said that the boogie-woogie was a rude example of where today's youth is headed!" They both giggle as the two follow one another around the room and across the decades.

Estelle slept well that night, dreaming of FDR shaking Bill Clinton's hand, Greta starring in a movie beside Robin Williams, and an entire nation rollerblading to Benny Goodman. And Mike? He slept peacefully, too. His was an exhausted slumber, much needed after valiantly trying to keep up with his grandmother on the dance floor all afternoon.

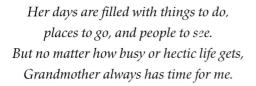

Her days are filled with things to do,
places to go, and people to see.
But no matter how busy or hectic life gets,
Grandmother always has time for me.

The Ballerina

*M*usic from a small record player paces her steps as she twirls and leaps beneath the wide archway. A ten-year-old's imagination transforms the space between the dining and living rooms into a stage. Her crinoline half-slip, pulled up under her arms and caught about the waist with a wide cinch belt, makes a stiff, ruffly tutu.

Seated in the rocking chair, Grandma does double duty as baby-sitter and an audience of one. Her gray head bobs gently in rhythm to the music.

The needle reaches the inner grooves on the old 78 record and sways with a dance of its own. With the dance done, Grandma bursts into enthusiastic applause. The ballerina accepts this praise with a deep curtsy.

"I always wanted to be a dancer," the old woman says, surprising her granddaughter.

She had never thought of Grandma in any way but aged with arthritis and wheezing from asthma. As Grandma talks of this hidden dream, however, stiff joints and labored breathing drift away to offer

a glimpse of a young girl with long, flowing hair the child had seen only in the old family album. She had danced secretly at night, the woman confides, barefoot in the wet grass, the darkness hiding the world from her clandestine dreams.

As these two talk and giggle, for an instant the ticks of time relent and a shadowy curtain parts. Two little girls—one from a faded photograph and the other in a makeshift tutu—reach across generations and share a dance of musical dreams.

She expresses herself in so many ways: in laughter and tears, in gentle words and firm hugs. Grandmother is a joyful contradiction; wise with years, yet forever a child at heart.

The Tides Inside

A chill runs through me as I step into the predawn darkness on the deck. My coffee steams as I cup it in my hands. The wooden benches are wet with the night's dew, so I stand by the railing, looking off into the still-shadowed patch of trees on the dunes that slope down to the lake. I can barely hear the roll and crash of the surf.

As long as I can remember, I have loved mornings like this—on vacation, here along the coast near Douglas, Michigan. And that has everything to do with Grandma.

Back in the early 1950s, every so often Grandma and Grandpa Davis used to take their daughter to this coast for vacations. This area was just being discovered then as a peaceful getaway from the urban busy-ness of Chicago.

Every-so-often visits soon became fairly frequent. The Davises enjoyed escaping the city to spend time as a family in this tranquility. They rented a lakefront cottage from a minister friend of theirs. My mom would dig in the sand and splash in the lake. Grandpa would just sit on the deck reading, soaking in the silence. Evenings were spent working puzzles and playing charades. And in the mornings, Grandma would take long walks on the beach.

By the time I was born—my parents' third (and last) child—the trips to Douglas had become an annual event. Some of my earliest memories are of evenings filled with cricket chirps and rising with the sun to explore on the beach with Grandma.

I remember once, when I was six, hopping down the cool dunes next to the wooden stairway leading to the lake, with Grandma following on the stairs. We walked along the shore, exploring as the sun come up over the dunes and trees. The lake looked like it was on fire. Holding my hand as we walked, she said, "You know, Johnny, I got so excited when I found out that your mother was having you. You really are a blessing."

I looked up at my grandma and saw that her eyes were shining as much as the sun on the lake. Then I looked down and saw a bright green stone! It was as smooth as the soft sand under our feet. As I crouched down and turned my treasure over and over in my fingers, Grandma stooped and said, "You know what that is, Johnny? It's glass. Many years ago, it could have been part of a pop bottle that fell into the lake. The water tosses it back and forth,

endlessly smoothing its jagged edges. And then, one day, the lake leaves it on the beach for some lucky young boy to find." Grandma smiled as we stood and I tucked the lucky glass stone into my pocket.

Every year we came back to the same stretch of beach. The minister eventually sold his vacation house, but we knew people throughout the community and always found a place to rent for a week each summer.

As I grew, I spent less time with sand castles and skipping stones. My older brother and sister were in college. They had summer jobs and only came up for a long weekend. My independence was expanding, and I found kids my own age in the town's ice cream parlors and video game arcades. Even when I was in high school, Grandma and I would take our morning walk, or as Grandma called it, "our waking stroll," on the beach.

"Have you ever noticed something about this place?" Grandma said one morning as we walked. "It's the same beach. Same lake. Same trees." And as we waved to the Petersons passing in their sailboat she added, "Even the same folks in the same boats. Yet, somehow it always seems different. Each time is fresh and new."

I looked around us. The trees are bigger, I thought. And the beach is much smaller now that the lake has risen. And we've changed. But it is always familiar, and new, to me. Grandma smiled and nodded and we kept walking, leaving a trail of footprints in the wet sand.

The summer after I graduated from college, Grandma and I shared a waking stroll that I will never forget. Since commencement, fears about facing the world for the first time had filled me. Important choices had to be made. The words that Grandma spoke to me that morning in July cast a crucial light on my future.

It was a morning like many others. But I felt closer to Grandma than I ever had before. I was now living in the world of adults.

We were walking along in silence, just before sunrise. Grandma turned her gaze to the sky. I followed her eyes and spotted the faint moon, still holding its nightly vigil. Then she said, "The tides of the lake have always fascinated me. Forces that we can't see act on the water—but we can see the effect."

Deep, I thought as I glanced over at Grandma. But now she was looking out at the water, lost in contemplation.

"No matter what people do, the tide will continue. It takes the sand that people try to replace. It rusts holes in the iron breakers along the beach. The water goes where it has to go," she paused and looked over at me, a straightforward gaze, adult to adult. "And you know what? We all have tides within ourselves as well. And we have to let the water go where it needs to go. Fighting the tides is a losing battle. Follow your dreams, John. Follow your tides."

I stopped walking and stared at this wise woman. Her words cleared my mind and instantly untied the knot in my stomach. How did she do that? She was smiling that smile at me and I could only smile back. Then, as I hugged her with the sun just rising, I said, "Thanks, Grandma."

The sky is just brightening now as I finish the last of my coffee. The sun is gently chasing the shadows from the trees. I can barely see the lake through the gaps in the branches. The rest of the family will be up tomorrow to spend another week here in Douglas, Michigan. But today is our time. I hear the door open and I turn and smile. It's Grandma.

"Ready for our waking stroll, Johnny boy?" she asks over her glasses.

"Anytime, Grandma," I reply, "anytime."

The Carrot Cake Gang

"What kind of business?" Bonnie asked.

"Catering. We're great cooks. With five of us working, this business will run itself." Edna was persuasive. Within an hour, The Carrot Cake Gang, a business owned by five "seventy-something" ladies, was born.

The group sent out flyers, and three jobs came their way.

"The 15th is my Bingo day," Norma announced, studying the calendar. "I can't help that day."

Edna waved a hand. "No problem. Four of us can handle the shower."

"My daughter's giving birth around the 20th," Doris added. "When she goes into labor, I'll have to go join her." Edna still wasn't concerned—until Bonnie tripped and wound up in a wheelchair the very same day Brenda announced a required appearance at a Social Security hearing scheduled for the 15th.

Now Edna was beginning to panic. Could she and Doris handle 25 bridal shower guests? Then the last chip was thrown. Doris's daughter went into labor on the 14th. Edna watched her last partner board a plane for Ohio.

Edna called her two daughters and her daughter-in-law, begging for help. But nobody had time on such short notice.

"I can help, Gram!" offered 12-year-old Jessica. "Mom says I can do it. Please! Let me help." Edna was desperate, so she agreed.

The following morning, Jess arrived. Edna looked like she was in shock. "Give me your menu," Jessica said, taking control. "I'll see if there's anything I've made before." Jess's confidence broke the ice and they began preparing some of the food. By day's end, the kitchen looked like a tornado had danced through it: Flour crowned

Edna's hair, powdered sugar decorated the floor, and every pot and bowl in the house was stacked in the sink.

Tucking an exhausted Jessica into her guest bed that night, Edna's back ached. What had she gotten herself into? Fortunately, Jessica was undaunted. She woke Edna with a breakfast tray the next morning. "Aren't you sick of the kitchen yet?" Edna laughed.

"I love cooking," Jessie enthused. "You know, Mom and Aunt Susan think your business is silly. They don't know how important it is for women to have meaningful work."

Edna stopped buttering her toast. "And you do?"

"Sure. I'm going to run my own business some day," Jess said casually. "Then you can help me. You're a pretty good worker." The comment made Edna laugh again, but Jess was perfectly serious.

"Having you in my life has always been a joy, but I'm just realizing how little I've appreciated you," Edna said. "When all of my partners ran out on me, I thought there'd be no way I could do it alone. Instead, I've found a partner with more enthusiasm than everyone else put together!" Jessica grinned and gave her grandmother a great, big hug.

Edna and Jess worked tirelessly in tandem, putting together a perfect shower. The next day, Edna calculated the profits after subtracting the cost of ingredients, then wrote her first salary check to Miss Jessica Palmer.

"Wow!" Jess exclaimed when Edna appeared at her front door with the check and a Carrot Cake Gang apron with "Jessica, Executive Chef," embroidered in green thread.

"You know, Grandma, I did this because I thought it would be fun. I wanted your business to succeed—not because I expected anything in return," said Jessica, admiring her new apron.

"Well, I can't let my new partner work without compensation," Edna said, "and the real reason I'm here is to check your schedule with your Mom. I'm informing my other partners you're onboard or they're all fired."

"Gram!"

"Now, Jess, women need meaningful work to make their lives complete. Isn't that what you taught me?"

Jessica grinned and hugged Edna. "So, when's our next party?"

Things Grandma Used to Say

This morning, as I mixed eggs and milk, dipped slices of bread, and plopped them into the skillet, I thought of Grandma. But we never dined on French toast at Grandma's table. We ate "fried bread" she cooked in her "spider."

Grandma used a lot of expressions I don't hear any-more. She parked the car in the "car-building" rather than a garage. A field "all blowed out" with flowers meant they were in full bloom. Potatoes that had not cooked long enough to be soft when tested with a fork "still had a bone in 'em."

I always giggled when she referred to an exceptionally tall man as a "long drink of water" or described a fun-filled occasion as "a big-eyed time."

Road signs from Grandma's day were "finger boards" because they were like fingers pointing the way. "Teardrops on the dishes" simply meant someone had not dried them well with the towel.

Her expressions were graphic with colorful colloquialisms from a bygone era. Although she has been gone for several years, I still feel a sparkle of her spirit when I see a field "all blowed out" with flowers or when I test an underdone potato. She lives in the words I hear in my mind, reflected in a world she has left behind.

Generations may divide us, but love unites my grandma and me.

Apples in Summer

"Waste not, want not," Grandmother Rose always used to say, "for a little can be a lot."

She and Grandpa George used to live in a little four-room house they had built in the midst of an unkempt five-acre orchard in central Indiana. The peach and apple trees certainly needed some care to get back up to speed, but Grandmother Rose could always see the value in some time well spent. After a few years, the overhauled orchard was producing plump peaches and crisp apples again, and they were in business.

The years passed fruitfully. Rose and George enjoyed a peaceful life on their Midwestern oasis. Gradually, Grandmother Rose started a few small gardens to complement the orchard, and she always got a pretty good yield. Corn, tomatoes, watermelons, and fat cucumbers sprouted out of that country dirt for all they were worth.

After Grandpa passed away, Grandmother Rose continued to manage the orchard and keep up the gardens, still drawing customers for miles. Holding true to her maxim, she never wasted anything, even making corn cob jelly and strangely tasty water-melon rind pickles.

Then, the year of the "Big Storm," I got a taste of what "a little" can really mean.

My parents, my three younger sisters, and I lived in a spacious two-story house a few hours south of Grandmother Rose. One early summer day, the sky darkened earlier than usual. From our back-yard, I saw it swirl into an eerie black-green—a color that strikes an uneasy chill in you. Still transfixed by the sky, I heard a siren wail and, almost at the same time, my mother calling frantically for me to get in the cellar.

As my mother and my sisters and I quietly shivered in the dark cellar, a fierce tornado shook the house by the foundation. The wind screamed, and tree limbs fell thundering to the ground. And then, suddenly: silence. By the time we surfaced from the basement, the storm had leveled our home and half of our small Indiana town. No one was hurt, but we were refugees.

Tearfully, we girls gathered up what belongings hadn't been destroyed or blown away, stuck them in a cardboard box, and got in the (fortunately intact) car. We cried all the way to Grandmother Rose's house, where we were to stay while our parents rebuilt the demolished house. They knew that rebuilding wasn't possible with us underfoot.

"But," I wondered to myself as we rode past endless cornfields, "how could we possibly all fit into Grandmother Rose's house?"

When we arrived, Grandma ushered each of us to our rooms. The two youngest, Rachel and Sandi, shared the sewing room, now divided by an old, white sheet on which Grandmother Rose had drawn pictures of apple trees, the sun, and a greeting in bright red, "Welcome!" Over the next few months, that sheet became a gallery to which we attached drawings, letters from our parents, pictures, and notes.

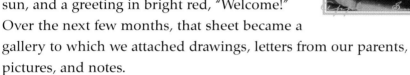

Jessie moved into the large closet beneath the stairs. Emptied of its usual mismatched items, it comfortably held a small cot, wooden peach-crate dressing table, and pictures cut from catalogs to serve as posters on the wall.

For me, Grandmother Rose had converted the enclosed back porch to a private room complete with a mattress on the floor piled with colorful pillows, a stack of books, and a reading lamp.

I would sometimes stay up late into the night reading those old, yellowing books. The old wringer-washer, pushed into the corner and covered with a quilt to double as a table, held Grandma's old, wooden radio.

If a little was not a lot, it certainly was enough to make us kids feel at home.

The next months really tested our creativity. Our big dollhouse at home had been blown to smithereens, but the one Grandmother Rose helped us make from shoe boxes, with thread-spool furniture and little people cut from magazines, was just the right size for carrying outdoors to play on blankets she spread beneath the apple trees. Fragrant white blossoms fluttered down on our miniature neighborhood like snow.

Even though there wasn't any extra money (or time, for Grandma had an orchard to run) for a vacation, in the languid days of August Grandmother Rose let the apples hang on the trees for a while, and we "traveled" to the back of the orchard and set up camp. For three days we cooked over a campfire (we even made a Dutch oven apple crisp!), slept on the ground, and listened to the frogs singing us to sleep at night.

On rainy days, we played in Grandma's small, tilting attic. We spent hours dressing up in old clothes and putting on plays. Grandma brought us fresh apple juice to sample and was always a willing audience.

Then—as sudden as that fateful storm—came the announcement that our house had been rebuilt. Our parents were on their way. It was time to go home.

"Time to get you out of this cramped place," our mother whispered apologetically the next day when she came to pick us up.

All she saw were makeshift rooms, Grandmother Rose's kitchen overflowing with apples, cider jugs, the cider press, and projects pushed into every corner. It had taken me a whole summer's worth of Grandma's "little into a lot" magic to see past these trivialities, so I didn't try to change my mother's mind on the car trip back home. Instead, my sisters and I insisted the following summer, and all those afterward, on going to Grandmother Rose's. We learned how to make all kinds of things out of apples: cider, pies, butter, jelly, dried rings, and even wrinkled apple dolls. We also learned how to run a business.

The time eventually came that Grandmother Rose needed our help in tending her orchard and taking care of her customers. And eventually, the business became ours. My sister Jessie and her family live there and run it to this day.

The ingenuity to turn a little into a lot is a good trait to have while rebuilding—a necessary task that the storms of life often demand. Now, as a grandmother myself, I often fall back on that bit of wisdom. And on those days when it seems like there just isn't enough to get me through, I like to make a fresh apple pie. The aroma takes me back to Grandmother Rose's house just long enough to hear her say again, "Easy, child, let's see what we can make from this."

Mix It and Roll It . . .

*W*hen I was five, my favorite things were my miniature rolling pin, my teeny, tiny pans, and my Grandma! She had silver hair—I don't remember it ever being any other color. She always wore an apron and had those funny, rolled-down nylons that circled her ankles like wrinkly sausages.

We would get up before sunrise to make coffee and sandwiches for Gramps to take to his construction job. Then Gram and I would sit and have "coffee" (mine was milk in a coffee cup) and plan dinner for the day. That always included dessert. Dessert was the finishing touch to every evening's meal. I think I knew how to make an apple pie before I knew how to boil water!

We would gather the ingredients and place them in a random circle on the countertop that was really a cabinet with a shiny white sink

attached to it. Then we would get my little red chair that I could stand on and place it next to Gram.

Measuring was never really measuring, but a bit of this and a handful of that and a scoop of the other. Everything went into the biggest bowl in Gram's kitchen. It had to be big because soon four hands began squishing and squeezing and smashing those unmeasured things together.

All the while, Gram would talk about all of the chores we would do that day after the baking was finished. We would make bread, start dinner, and then later we would wash clothes and hang them out to dry on the clothesline we had strung in a triangle between two poles and the old hickory tree.

Then she placed a handful of dough in front of me, dusted my counter space with flour, and we rolled and rolled that dough until it was thin—but not too thin! Then we fit the crusts into the two pie pans, one for each of us.

We peeled, cored, washed, and cut the apples—millions of them. I think they were as big as grapefruits! And, amazingly, all of those apple slices fit into the pans. Then we threw in some sugar, chunks of butter, cinnamon, more flour, and just a pinch of salt.

While we rolled out the tops of our pies, Gram piped in her squeaky, off-key singing voice, "We mix it, and roll it, and pop it in a pan. . . . " Then we covered those apples and popped the pans into the oven and moved on to the next chore.

From that point in the day, whatever we did was accented with the scent of those baking pies, the big one and my little one. It was a fragrant, sweet reminder of the tasty treat that was to come. After they baked for what seemed like hours (and she always knew just when), Gram opened the oven and apple pie perfume filled the kitchen in a blast of heat. She wrapped a towel around her hands and pulled the pies out to cool. They were always perfect and steam-ing and oh, did they smell wonderful!

They tasted heavenly, but eating them never compared to creating them (although you'd never know from Gramps, the way he'd "ooh" and "ahh" over the pie's delicate flavor). My favorite part was always standing next to Gram, on my little red chair, with my miniature rolling pin.

Scraps

"**B**unny needs new stuffing and a patch."

It was midnight when Martha heard those words, spoken by her granddaughter as she stood on the other side of the screen door. The 18-year-old held up a dilapidated cloth animal. "Do you have any scraps?"

"Oh my," said Martha to herself as she gathered the stick-thin young lady with neon-pink hair into her arms, "this child needs a bit of patching up, too."

Melinda had finally made the leap from the edge of a perilous life to the safety of Grandma's house.

After phoning her parents to say that she was fine, not coming home, and not with her boyfriend, Melinda allowed her grandmother to tuck her into bed on the couch.

"Tomorrow, we'll clean out the sewing room upstairs and make you a place in there," Martha promised.

The older woman had just fallen asleep when she awoke and heard Melinda crying and talking in her sleep. Martha sat on the steps and tried to decipher what the child was saying; she didn't want to wake her and broach the child's torment until she was ready.

The next day, they worked hard in the sewing room. Afterward, Melinda took a nap, ate very little supper, and took Bunny upstairs to keep her company in bed.

"Tomorrow we'll find a patch for Bunny," Martha promised, calling after her.

But that night, Melinda's nightmare woke them both.

Martha found her granddaughter in the kitchen. Without her dark makeup, Melinda looked so young and vulnerable. Martha tried to peer through Melinda's pink bangs and into the girl's sad eyes.

"I need my sleep, child. Tell me what's got us both awake," said Martha, sprinkling sugar on some bread for cinnamon toast.

"Big clocks are after me," said Melinda, trying to laugh through the brimming tears. "I'm afraid of tomorrow. All of my tomorrows. I have too many decisions: college, marriage, work, moving, staying home." A long pause followed.

"I guess mother probably told you about some of my yesterdays," Melinda finally said in a barely audible voice.

"Some of them. Why don't you tell me about the others," Martha invited, sliding the plate of toast toward her granddaughter.

As she talked, Melinda absently nibbled around the edges of a piece of toast. Like a bunny, Martha thought to herself, remembering the day many years before when they had made hot chocolate and cinnamon toast and then invited the stuffed pet to their "party." That day, Melinda's problems had been easily fixed; tonight's were made of darker stuff. *But none so bad*, Martha thought, *that they couldn't be mended.*

Melinda kissed the top of her grandmother's head as she yawned her way back up to the sewing room. "Grandma, tomorrow let's patch Bunny."

In the morning, Melinda came downstairs with the bags of quilt scraps. Martha had her sort through them at the kitchen table.

"This is the Christmas dress you made me when I was in kinder-garten!" Melinda cried, pulling out a square of crimson-plaid taffeta. Martha picked up a flowered fabric. "These were curtains for your tree house. This one," she said, holding up a lavender lace, "was your junior bridesmaid's dress when Aunt Laura got married. You grew two inches between the day when I cut it out and the wedding. See, I had to let down the hem."

"I can't believe you kept all the scraps," mused Melinda.

"I've been planning a quilt of your life since before you were born," explained Martha. "I just haven't gotten around to piecing it together."

"Can we, you know, maybe do it in a small quilt? To hang on my wall," said Melinda, hesitantly.

"My wall"—college, home, or a working girl's apartment? Martha wondered to herself. "Why, that would look real nice," she said.

They worked for the next few weeks connecting pieces of this and that into a thing of beauty. All the while, they talked, laughed, and even cried a time or two. One day, Martha heard Melinda on the phone; a few days later, packages began arriving from colleges. Melinda began adorning herself with one of her grandfather's old dress shirts she'd found in the rag bag. She'd washed and ironed it and wore it tied around her waist. Her nightmares lessened, much to

Martha's relief. Like the quilt coming to life under their hands, Melinda seemed to be piecing together her life, bit by bit.

"How about adding this?" Melinda held up a small square of black leather. "I cut up my pants—to make Bunny a new collar," she said sheepishly.

Martha smoothed it with her gnarled fingers. "Let's embroider the date on it," she suggested casually, "in pink thread, perhaps?"

"The color of my hair?" Melinda couldn't decide whether to puff up like a wet hen and take offense or laugh, matching the smile hiding behind her grandmother's innocent remark.

"Why, of course, child," said Martha. "It's the pink I look for in every sunrise. It's one of my favorites—the color of tomorrow."

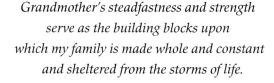

Grandmother's steadfastness and strength
serve as the building blocks upon
which my family is made whole and constant
and sheltered from the storms of life.

Past, Present: Perfect

I watch my grandmother watch my daughter—one life already turning the fourth corner, the other barely focused on her first. And I wonder: What strengths, foibles, and characteristics will my daughter inherit? I wonder if we have time—time for my baby to know her great-grandmother. I hope so. Although my daughter will enjoy positive role models—in my own mother and, I hope, myself—I wish her some time with my Grandma. She is the beginning, to me, of a powerful lineage.

Grandma grew up poor, in a cold-water flat on Chicago's south side. Really, she raised herself, because her mother needed to work day and night. Her father, well, his name just simply never came up. But despite such hardship, my grandmother grew up strong and wise and generous. She didn't take any flack and insisted that all the rules

of rationality be followed. I often wonder that if she'd been given a different birth year—something closer to the 1980s—how high she could have flown.

Grandma passed on to my own mother her refusal to give in to adversity. "Problem . . . solution," my mother always says. My mom has a slightly more dogmatic approach than Grandma, but the philosophy remains the same. Perhaps Mom's straight-to-the-point tactics are what Grandma would have chosen if she, like her daughter, had entered and succeeded in the business world. When I wonder how high Grandma could have climbed, maybe I see the answer in Mom.

As for my own inheritance, I too received an instinctive ability to conquer adversity. I have a slightly more seek-and-ye-shall-find attitude, more open-minded and less pragmatic than my mother, but nonetheless a direct descendent of both Grandma's and Mom's ideas. I suppose my less stringent outlook makes me appear like a textbook product of my generation—one foot placed in my career, the other in my family's concerns, and both legs dancing a little jig to balance the act.

Today, I look at my beautiful baby girl. She probably won't experience hardship like my grandmother. She will face fewer power struggles to make her mark, like my mother. She has a progressive history. But she will face obstacles. That's just life.

But as she faces those trials, I hope she sees within herself this inherited ability to conquer life's little and big hurdles. Let my grandmother's ability to beat the odds filter down through the generations and enter my daughter's soul. If she possesses my grandmother's strength of character, I know she'll be all right.

And I do have proof. I see it reflected in the eyes and smiles of my grandmother, my mother, and myself as we gaze at the tender stirring of my daughter in her great-grandmother's arms.

Her joy is ageless. Her wisdom is timeless. Her love is priceless. Grandmother is like a precious gem that emits a brilliant and eternal glow.

The Stories Grandma Can Tell

*W*hen an old person dies, a saying goes, it's like burning down a library. Grandmothers are not only a reliable source for family facts, but they are also brimming with wonderful tales about the storied days of yore.

Fortunately for Vi's grandchildren, she happily shares her tales—some a little taller than others—from when she was young. When the time is right for Grandma Vi to start, the kids all gather around. Legs are tucked under quilts, steaming mugs of hot cocoa appear, and now everyone is all ears. Even the adults lean in and listen to the tall tales that only Grandma Vi can spin.

"I grew up in a remote part of the country where farms were a brisk breeze apart," begins Grandma Vi, taking a sip out of her mug. "There was never a glimpse of a cheery light in a neighbor's window to offer any kindly reassurance on a pitch-black night.

"My three cousins and I were left alone while my parents were away for a night. Stevie, a sturdy girl of 14, was left in charge. Frank and I were both 11. Little Tad was nine, but was quick to tell anyone that he was, 'goin' awn ten.'" The kids all laugh (and even Grandma Vi can't suppress a smile) as she squeaks the high voice of little Tad.

"The daylight hours passed quickly as we basked in the heady feeling of being in charge," she continues, suddenly serious again looking slowly at each set of bright eyes. "As the yellow sun dropped to orange and red, however, dusk brought a sense of dread. We hurried to finish our chores before darkness could catch us outside, then rushed into the house to light the lamp. Four sets of eyes nervously watched as the last traces of day slipped into night.

"Silence crept into the room like the creak of a floorboard that jerks your eyes open after everyone is in bed," and Grandma Vi imitates her own "crrreeeaaak" as the kids all giggle and shriek. "Our isolation felt spooky, and, in a burst of bravado, Frank started telling a ghost story. One story led to another, with each child taking turns—even Tad tried—as we made supper. The stories and the supper soothed our spirits—somewhat. Each of us occasionally glanced quickly outside, or off to a dark corner of the room.

"The soft glow from the lamp's flame cast our shadows high against the walls and reflected off the window by the sink. Sounds of forks

scraping and plates clinking slowly replaced speech. Then I shuddered a shake as I saw a strange form out of the corner of my eye," and Grandma Vi's eyes stretch as wide as saucers, "outside the big window by the sink. Suddenly I was too scared to blink. I nudged Frank and silently gestured toward the shadowed form on the other side of the glass. The mood in the room was tight enough to sway any which way, and Frank had turned whiter than milk.

"The immobile shadow looked like a huge head, too big to be human. My chest was tight, and I realized that I had been holding my breath because I was afraid to breathe. My heart beat so hard that the expression 'scared to death' suddenly came alive for me.

"Stevie and Tad caught our silent stare and now everyone was as still as the shadow. Nobody dared speak. The clicks of the ticking clock raised the fear a notch." And Grandma Vi adds her own "tick tock, tick tock," drawing the quiet a little tighter.

"Then, all four of us leaped off our seats and made tracks through the door to the family room. The shadow simultaneously released a bellow that matched our screams! Moooarrrawwwahhhh!" blasts

Grandma as the kids unwittingly play the part of the screams. Then, with a single hand up for quiet, everyone is still.

"Then, just as fast: silence.

"As our heartbeats slowed, confidence started to grow. Stevie led the way back to the kitchen. The shadow was gone, but the ticking clock was still keeping its watch. Curiosity led us outside, but now the night didn't seem to hold as much fright.

"We made our way around the yard and noticed that we had left the barnyard gate gaping in our haste to get inside. As I walked up to the fence, I saw a cow watching me closely. 'Closer than a cow usually chooses to stare,' I thought, as I latched the gate closed.

"Then all four of us scampered back indoors, locked the door, and drew the shades down tight. Every light was lit in the house that night. And," said Grandma Vi with a sly smile, "when my parents came home the next day, you can bet that we sure let them know that they were missed while they were away!"

"Tell it again!" her grandchildren urge time and time again, for there are no stories quite like the ones Grandma can tell. And she always tells it, as only Grandma Vi can do.

Beach Buddies

I can still smell Gram's southern home. . . . The summer morning mist tinged with the scent of white gardenias rising past dangling Spanish moss.

And then I would catch a whiff of bacon. Breakfast was already frying up in the pan by seven o'clock. Thick-cut bacon mixed with grits and—believe it or not—Coca Cola! (not from a can or a plastic liter bottle, but from the small green bottle). Gram even had an opener attached to the wall. By breakfast, she would already be dressed in her flowered bathing suit. Gram always had beautiful, shapely, tanned legs. And they were always tan—year round.

As far as Gram was concerned, the only meal that needed to be prepared in the kitchen during the summer was breakfast. That's because Gram was a bona fide beach bum!

Each summer day, after breakfast, we would go through the routine of packing up sandwiches and sodas, getting ice for the cooler, fetching towels, pails, shovels, and little chairs for each of us—six of them with small umbrellas attached.

We were like little ants preparing for winter: scurrying about, gathering our food and supplies to get through the long stretch. Except our stretch was to be a fun, sun-filled day at the beach!

Gram's lyrical voice would firmly encourage us in our preparations. "Now come awn, y'all, put yah drawers on and jump in the cah. Don't maysh theym san'wiches. No one'll touch theym if they's all mayshed up!"

We would all pile in her big station wagon and drive the seemingly endless journey across bridge after bridge, some of them lifting and some turning and always "just one more." The open windows wafted warm, salty air on us as we neared the ocean.

Finally, the wagon would come to a stop along graceful, white mounds of sand peppered with reeds of grass. We would pile out onto the hot, sandy pavement and dash through the dunes, kicking up sand as we ran and squealed with delight. We would drop our bags in a heap and race toward the crashing surf. We chased the waves, and the waves chased us back. And, laughing, we did it again. Then we would run back to the base camp, which Gram had already staked out.

The chairs were anchored in the sand, and the umbrellas were an open refuge from the glaring sun. Then we would run back to the wet sand by the water and plop down and begin digging. Already, by only ten o'clock we were covered with an invisible layer of salt that we could taste by licking our lips. Splotched with spots of sand, our skin began collecting deep shades of color, just like Gram's.

We would grab our pails and race up the shoreline, Gram leading the way in search of water-borne treasures: intact and broken shells; smooth, colored glass; and slimy seaweed—all of which we used for the sand castle fortress that always got washed away.

In the afternoon, Gram tied chunks of meat to strings by the shore and we would wait impatiently for the crabs to tiptoe out of the ocean. When one would finally come to bite, we would jump up and down as Gram plucked it up with a swift sweep of her hand. Gram sure knew how to catch crabs!

Then we buried Gram in the sand. She would laugh, "Oh my Laud, oh my Laud," throwing back her head, her hazel eyes twinkling with delight. She slowly sunk deeper into the great hole on the beach that took forever to dig with those six little shovels and the waves washing in. Finally, she was sufficiently swallowed up by the sand and . . . all too soon, it was time to rinse off all the sand, load up the car, and trace our way back across all of those bridges. And Gram would remind us that tomorrow would be here soon, and, without doubt, we would be back at the beach again.

Coach

The view from Timothy's bedroom window changed all the time, but somehow it always remained the same.

It was always other people: other people going about their lives; other 11-year-olds shooting baskets, playing games of "HORSE" and "one-on-one," and running the full-court press. He watched every televised game and knew the playing styles of the teams almost as well as the coaches knew them. He really loved basketball.

But Timothy didn't go anywhere—except to the doctor. His legs had been paralyzed in a swimming accident four years ago. Teachers and physical therapists came to visit him frequently, but they'd given up trying to convince his parents that he would be able to do more.

His parents tried to keep him entertained: video games, a big-screen television, a computer with e-mail. He'd made friends on the Internet, but none of them knew that he was a prisoner. He'd thought of sending an "SOS" into cyberspace, saying that he was

held captive by some mean people. But he wasn't a captive, and he knew that his parents weren't mean. They were, as they told him a dozen times a week, just concerned for his safety. "It's for your own good," they said.

They were trying the same "for your own good" tactics with his grandma, Anna. She'd had a major heart attack and was coming to stay until they could get her into a nursing home. Timothy wasn't sure if Grandma Anna knew about that.

It was hard to imagine her not in her home, but at least she'd be company for him. Maybe he could teach her how to play video games.

"Don't expect too much," his mother cautioned the night before Grandma Anna arrived. "She's an old, sick lady. We have to take care of her."

Grandma Anna immediately had other ideas. She insisted on bringing her old cat, Tatters, and a stationary bicycle with her. She had her daughter put the bike in Timothy's room since his was the biggest. She winked at him as if they shared a secret. And before the first week was out, they did. Grandma Anna had "hired" Timothy as her personal bicycling coach. She showed him how to hook up the bike's odometer and set up a record-keeping system in a notebook.

When he read the odometer's number to enter it in his book, he thought he'd made a mistake or that the machine was broken. It said 9,200 miles.

"Have you really been this far, Grandma Anna?"

"Farther. This is just as far as I've counted."

"How long did it take?"

"About five years. Every day except when I was in the hospital. I had heart trouble as a child and was not expected to live very long," she told her grandson, "and I certainly had no intention of 'traveling' this far. And if I'd thought about it ahead of time, I might not have started. But now I cover six miles in about 45 minutes per 'ride.' It's easy. And," she smiled, "I've discovered I'm not a quitter."

Timothy and his grandmother were soon beginning each day with the bicycle odometer clicking, clicking, clicking. She didn't want to watch TV while she biked, she said, suggesting instead that Timothy "work out" with her.

"But I can't walk," he protested. "I can't ride a bike."

"You can ride a wheelchair," she responded from her bike, huffing and puffing in a steady rhythm. "Look at me, I'm not really going anywhere on this thing, but that doesn't keep me from moving along," huff, puff, "one mile at a time. And don't tell your folks, but I'm not going to be moving on to a nursing home either."

Pretty soon, Timothy was making intricate "wheelie" moves with his wheelchair, and he was lifting weights. He'd also looked up "sports for the disabled" on the Internet and asked his tutor how to get himself back into public school.

Grandma Anna talked the local Senior Citizens Center into getting exercise bikes, and convinced some of her sedentary friends to get on them.

"One mile at a time," she prods. She's a veteran now, having logged more than 30,000 miles. "My coach and I used to say that 'life can be a freewheeling adventure when everyone else has given up,'" says Anna with a wink from the seat of her bike.

Grandma Anna sometimes organizes field trips to senior athletic events with the occasional side trip to wheelchair basketball games. The starting forward for the local college team is a wiry, blond pre-law student named Timothy.

"My coach," says Anna, pointing proudly. And Timothy calls his grandmother the same.

Midnight Gardener

*W*e're giving small bags of potpourri for Christmas this year. We gathered the leaves and petals from Gamma Sandy's secret garden.

Our parents should've known better than to put her in a nursing home before she was ready. They also should've checked to see if the windows locked. Then again, most people wouldn't think that old ladies would climb out a window to plant a garden.

But our Gamma Sandy did.

She ordered seeds and a trowel from the home shopping channel. As soon as they arrived, she began her covert planting.

Somebody had bulldozed a shed behind the maintenance and storage buildings, leaving bare dirt. Gamma had seen it and thought, as she confided later, "it had the makings of a real nice garden."

It took her a week of midnight plantings, but by the time I discovered what she was up to, she'd sowed hollyhocks, sweet peas, daisies, cosmos, marigolds, and sunflowers.

The nursing home grew concerned about her that week and called our parents. "She sleeps all day," they fretted, talking as if she weren't sitting there dozing right under their noses.

It was the dirt under her fingernails that gave her away.

I poked my brother in the ribs and pointed. That's the way Gamma's hands looked when she lived in her house with the gardens.

"Gamma, have you been digging?" I whispered while the others debated her possible affliction.

She opened one eye. "Y'all have to help me. I'm getting too old to crawl around on my hands and knees all night."

As Gamma's oldest grandchild, I commanded a little attention when I suggested that perhaps Gamma was still adjusting to her new surroundings. It had taken me weeks to get used to living in a dormitory at college, I explained. "Let's wait and see before hauling Gamma off to the hospital for tests. I'm home for the summer and can check on her."

"Me, too," chimed in my younger brother, a senior in high school. I knew we could rope in our sisters.

As if on cue, Gamma sprung completely awake, charming the family and staff into leaving her alone. After supper, we came back and took Gamma for a walk. Sure enough, there was Gamma's garden.

"The rows are pretty straight, considering that I dug them in the dark," she said proudly. "But I could use some herbs in that corner, and a rose bush would be so nice. I worry about those rocks along the back edge. They need to come out."

Before we knew it, we were at the garden center spending Gamma's money on the plants she'd listed.

That night, we got everything she'd ordered in the ground. (We told our parents that we were going to help a friend with a project.) Gamma sneaked out to oversee our planting. Over the weeks, she taught us how to cultivate, weed, hoe, thin, fertilize, transplant, and

harvest early blooms . . . all by the glow of our flashlights and the light of the moon.

"Gamma," I asked one night while resting from all of the hoeing I'd been doing, "doesn't anybody notice the garden?"

She threw back her head with a gentle laugh, her hair a silvery halo in the moonlight. "I tell one person it's somebody else's garden, and I tell that one it's so-and-so's. Nobody wants to admit that they don't know what's going on, so they don't ask."

All summer we worked, Gamma sitting on a chair that we brought. During our parents' visits, Gamma even showed them the garden. More than one staff person was willing to take credit for such a lovely spot for the old folks to enjoy.

Gamma had to do most of the final harvesting of petals and leaves for the Christmas potpourri. I was back in college, and the others were busy with school. I sent Gamma a college sweatshirt to wear on her late-night forays. The garden needed to be cleaned off for winter, and I was sorry I wasn't around. I figured that would be the end of it.

Not for Gamma. She made a deal with the nursing home: If they got someone to till "their" garden, she'd teach gardening to the residents come spring. They could even start seeds in those little window boxes, she said. She enlisted reinforcements from fellow residents: a former flower judge itching to get her fingers back in the posies and a gentleman farmer who volunteered to plant bottle gourds to make into birdhouses during the winter for next year.

Gamma, of course, continued to do the bulk of the work (and occasional skulduggery).

In a letter I received before Thanksgiving, she told of planting daffodil bulbs in the moonlight. "I never would have guessed that this garden could have come so far. And I have you kids to thank for that," she wrote in her looped script. "This cycle of life that is gardening really keeps me going."

And then at the end of her letter she wrote: "The spirit persists even when the body resists." A delicate rose petal was taped on the corner of the page, reminding me that love reaps a rich harvest.

Grandma is a cornucopia of treasures and our bountiful harvest of joy.

Home Is Where the Heart Is

*A*t college one year, I discovered a tiny green tree frog far from home, hopping across the hot cement in a grocery store parking lot. Gingerly, I picked him up and brought him to my apartment. I made a terrarium out of an old aquarium by adding a small, shallow dish of water, some dirt, and a few plants. Then I brought him crickets and other insects, which he eagerly devoured. I guess I came by the love of all creatures naturally—through my grandmother's example.

Years ago, Grandma Margie instilled in me a love for all living things. She carried an easy air of compassion around her wherever she went. She always said that in life you must try to respect all the other lives around you and try to spread as much love as you can. Those two words have really stuck with me: respect and love.

The summer that I turned nine, Grandma Margie asked me to stay with her for a couple of weeks when her German shepherd, Blackie, was unable to nurse all of her eleven pups. I was thrilled to help Grandma feed the puppies. I cut the tip of the nipple off of one of my old doll's bottles so that the milk would flow faster. One by one, we fed each eager puppy, going through the procedure around the clock. I didn't even mind getting up at two o'clock in the morning to feed them.

"Be careful with them," Grandma had said, "they're just like babies." I remember holding each squirming puppy longer than I needed, just to observe the miracle of a new life. I'd often let several of them curl up in my lap and watch them snuggle off to sleep.

Later, what a joy it was to watch the puppies' eyes open. When they took their first uneasy steps, we sat on the grass beside them. I giggled watching the puppies learn to assert themselves. The one I named Big Red fell backward every time he barked.

I was heartbroken when we had to give the puppies away. They all had become so precious to me. But Grandma said that it was our duty to let these little bundles of energy go off to new homes.

"That way," Grandma said, "we're able to spread even more joy around. Each one of these pups will be a loving companion to somebody new."

As we sat there in the grass that day, with the furry puppies crawling all over each other and us, Grandma said, "You know, animals are smart. They know when someone loves them." There was a twinkle in Grandma's eye as she added, "and I think they can sense a loving heart—that's why they find me."

I've found that to be true for me as well. Animals still have a way of finding Grandma and me. It seems that love is a magnet that is stronger than we can know, and its power continues to grow.

It is a fortunate grand-child who appreciates her grandmother's wisdom in the present rather than the past.

Betsy's Tales

When I was growing up in northern Georgia, I used to sit at Grammy's oval table. A well-used oak table, it boasted two leaves and stood on four sturdy legs. I didn't like to call Grammy eccentric, but when it came to that table, there really wasn't any doubt. She was. She'd pat that old table and say, "Your great-grandmother left me Ol' Betsy. You know, she's seen everything from my diapers down to your baby bottles. Yep, she's been faithful." Then Grammy would launch into one of her stories.

"Did I ever tell you about the time your granddad tried to fry fish?" she asked.

Oh yeah, I remembered it well. I'd probably heard all of her stories a dozen times, but there was always room for one more time. But before I could say yes, she would already be off . . .

"Well, let me tell ya. We had just gotten married and moved into the old house in town. You know the one, with that hulking, rusted-out Oldsmobuick sittin' in the yard now. Next to the Fletcher brothers' place. Anyhow, one day Granddad caught a mess of fish at a pond and brought 'em home for supper. One of the younger nephews—

Bobby, I think it was—was sittin' at Betsy across from the stove writing an essay for school while I was out pickin' a few tomatoes from the garden.

"Now hear this: Believing he was helping, Granddad poured a puddle of oil into the cast iron skillet and turned up the fire. After giving Bobby instructions to tell me, Granddad settled down in the living room to read the newspaper. Within a few minutes, Bobby starts a hollerin' from the kitchen, 'Fire! Fire!'

"I raced inside lickety-split just in time to see Granddad grab the skillet and put it under running water. But that kicked the flames up and in seconds, the blue gingham curtains were in flames. Granddad grabbed the curtain rod—his face all horrified and lit up—trying to save the burning curtains. He raced outside, threw the curtains to the ground and stomped the fire out. That was the last time Granddad ever got near my kitchen," finished Grammy with a chuckle, turning to fill the sun tea pitcher.

It seemed as though Grammy spent her whole life at that table (uh, I mean, Betsy).

It became the focal point when Sarah, the oldest granddaughter, got married. Family members gathered around Betsy to chat and make rice packets tied with blue ribbons to toss on Sarah's special day. The reception at Grammy's boasted a three-tiered wedding cake topped with confectionery roses. Grammy proudly placed the cake smack in the middle of Betsy. Six months later when the marriage fell apart, Betsy held the tears of the disenchanted bride and Grammy. I'm sure if Betsy could have, she would have wept right along with them.

After every Christmas, Grammy's table was sprinkled with all sorts of scraps of wrapping paper and spilled cranberry sauce and dressing. There always seemed to be one glum-faced grandchild who sat at the table pouting tearfully because he didn't get just want he wanted. Grammy would pull a chair up to Betsy and soothe the sorrow—usually with a slice of her blueberry pie and a kiss to chase the crying away.

Grammy especially felt a bond with her table when Betsy entered her golden years and, like Grammy, began to sag in the middle. One day, a grandkid crunching crackers into tomato soup noticed his bowl slipping toward the middle. "Grammy," he said, "my soup's running away!"

Grammy laughed. "You know what? Ol' Betsy still has a trick or two up her sleeve!"

Indeed, Betsy had endured ages of banging plastic cups and spilled drinks and silverware scrapes (lots of little hands can sure do some damage). Children turned to grandchildren, and soon enough, Betsy began to take on a forlorn look.

It was then that Grammy knew it was time to give up her beloved friend. One day, she dusted the crumbs from Betsy and wiped her down with an oiled cloth. Then she said goodbye. A couple of us carried the table to the backyard for a garage sale.

When a young couple stopped by looking for a dining table, Grammy showed off Ol' Betsy. She was sure that Betsy would be sturdy enough for a small family.

"How much do you want for the table?" asked the pregnant woman. Grammy studied the couple with that sensitive stare that could strip any pretension bare. "Go ahead," she said, her voice slightly cracking, "you can have her. I want her in a home where memories are still being made."

I would like to tell you the reason for my grandmother's success: Patience.

Lovely Advice

The day I became a wife, I was a bundle of nerves. For no apparent reason, I would burst into tears and fly off the handle. My mother, a pillar of strength that day—as always—somehow managed to get me dressed, coiffed, and made-up.

My father, who is not known for his comforting hugs and soothing words, even stopped by the dressing room to stroke my cheek and whisper, "I love you." (Oh, don't get me wrong. Dad's a great guy. But my sisters and I usually call on him for his rousing rendition of "On Top of Old Smoky"—not for tender thoughts before special events.)

Just as I passed through my fourth or fifth meltdown—my left shoe had suddenly, mysteriously disappeared—Grandma Joyce came into my room. Now Joyce is a no-nonsense grandmother. And she was fairly appalled at the mess I'd created: tissue paper everywhere,

79

loose articles of clothing scattered about, and eight jasmine-scented candles burning from any empty space on every flat surface. (The woman at the store had told me that jasmine had soothing qualities—perfect for quieting jangled nerves. Outside of straight-out voodoo, I was open to any tranquilizing options this afternoon.)

"My goodness," Joyce said with a frown. "We'd better set another six places for dinner, because sure as my name is Joyce Anne O'Donnell, there will be a fire and we will have a troop of uninvited firemen showing up. Annie, where is your pretty young head this afternoon?"

My grandmother usually said what she meant and meant what she said. My three sisters and I had long since learned to heed her words. I obediently blew out a few candles. "Grandma, I don't know what's wrong with me today. I can barely remember my last name."

"Well, see how lucky you are! In about two hours, you're going to change your last name anyway. So, let's cross that worry off the list," said Joyce in her calm, rapid-fire manner. "Now, do you have something old, something new, something borrowed, and something blue? It's an old superstition, your Grandma knows that, but it's tradition. Indulge me."

Taking a quick inventory, I counted my dress as something new, my mother's diamond earrings as something borrowed (she'd promised me I could wear these earrings on my wedding day—ever since I was four!), and the obligatory wedding garter as something blue. Something old was missing! I panicked.

Joyce reached into her pocket and pulled out a beautiful pearl necklace. My grandmother was forever pulling magic from her dresses. Every dress she owned had deep, fruitful pockets, and right at that moment, I clearly remember wondering how she managed to find a formal gown with concealed pockets beside each hip . . .

Right in the middle of that necklace hung a larger pearl in a platinum teardrop setting. Surrounding the pearl were tiny white diamonds. She offered the necklace to me. I hadn't planned on wearing a necklace, even though my gown offered the perfect frame for one—with a deep neckline fading into off-the-shoulder satin sleeves. Mom thought my neck bones, strong shoulders, and freckle-free chest were among my prettiest features, and that I should leave them unadorned. But the necklace, with its simple drama, somehow seemed appropriate.

"My mother gave me this necklace on the day I got married," Joyce explained. "With it she gave me some sound advice. She told me it was old, yes, but that I should never forget its beauty. Sort of like how you might feel in about five years . . . when you're down on your knees scrubbing the kitchen floor, with two babies crying for dinner, and your husband is late coming home from work.

"It's all going to seem very old and tiring and hardly worth it. But when that happens—and it will, mind you—you remember how much you love this man you're marrying today. You remember how something new will eventually turn into something old, and 'old' can mean worn out or, just as easily, it can mean warm and wise and comfortable. You'll have choices, Annie. Keep your eyes open for the wise ones."

I remember thinking, "Well, I would never be down on my knees scrubbing floors if I could help it. And the two crying babies—we'll have to see about that. . . . " But I was wise enough to realize that all these points were of secondary importance. And now that I think about it, Grandma Joyce gave me two wonderful old things that afternoon. She gave me a beautiful antique necklace, which I proudly wore, and she gave me a piece of sage advice, which I've worn in my heart every day since.

Like Mother, Like Daughter

It was an emotionally stormy evening and everyone took cover. The cat dove under the bed. The four-year-old twins uncharacteristically entertained themselves with building blocks. Jim disappeared into his study, relinquishing his usual "I-am-Father-and-I-rule" role. A storm was churning inside the Brewster home.

Emma Brewster, sweet 16 and full of life, had introduced her parents to an interesting young man named Ted the night before. Karen, Emma's mother, was not pleased. The boy was older—at least 20. He had tiny gold balls randomly placed in holes all over his body. He was a musician. Enough said.

Emma and Karen went back and forth, the mother shouting, "You will not date that boy!" And then the daughter yelling back, "I will date him, and you can't stop me!"

After about an hour, the storm retreated. Everyone knew, though, that the lingering clouds only meant a reprieve. Emma sat in her bedroom, chewing her lip and plotting rebellion. Karen stomped around the kitchen, moving through the after-dinner cleanup. But she was obviously gathering force to unleash another squall. She was determined to put a stop to Emma's relationship with Ted.

Karen's mom just sat in the living room, listening as usual. After all, she was only a guest in town for the week—just a visitor. What could she do? Besides, she could recognize that her daughter had passed the point of logical discussion. And her granddaughter had definitely crossed the state line of reason. There certainly was a family resemblance in these women.

So, biding her time—a concept only seasoned persons seem to understand—this old-fashioned woman waited for her moment. Then she went upstairs to Emma's room and knocked only once, "It's Gramma, honey. Can Gramma come in?"

"Gramma, pleeeeaze. Not now." But despite the words, the door opened a crack. "Your daughter is so stubborn. She thinks she can control my whole life. Well, she can't. I can date whoever I want."

"Where have I heard those words before?" Gramma mused. "Oh, yes. It was about 25 years ago. What a night! I'm glad your grandfather isn't here to tell the story. Until the day the good Lord took him, he never would discuss that night. He just couldn't talk about it."

Emma feigned disinterest. Arms crossed, she turned to the wall and rolled her eyes. But then she glanced back and said, "Gramma, you don't understand at all."

"Oh, but I do," the grandmother responded, welcoming Emma's bait. "And to tell the truth, I'm not surprised you're attracted to musicians. Your mother once went out with a musician, and your grandfather forbade the relationship. Your mother locked herself in her room for days."

Taking her granddaughter's hand, Gramma sat on the edge of the bed and led the way down memory lane. Gramma described how this mystery musician had looked: He had a thick mop of hair on his head and he wore cheap, brightly colored clothes. She described his philosophy: He believed in total freedom (unless that meant staying in school), and he thought love-ins and sit-ins would bring eternal peace. She described how her daughter thought she was madly in love.

"What happened then, Gramma?" asked Emma, fascinated, waiting for more.

"The boy left with his fellow band members. They went rambling off on a tour in a rumbling, smoky microbus. But the point is, your mama isn't just being stubborn, Emmy. She sees herself in you. She knows about broken hearts and romantic adventures. Maybe your young man is different, but you'll need to ease your mama into it. While you're at it, ease yourself in as well. If this is real, it will last."

Emma seemed to be thinking, mulling over the words just said. Her eyes were turned down now—arms no longer crossed. And to her grandmother, that meant progress. Now if she could only get a simi-lar response when she retold the very same story down in the kitchen! Sometimes a stubborn mule needed to be reminded of trails already traversed.

As she turned to leave Emma with her thoughts, the young girl grabbed her hand.

"Was he really a musician?" asked Emma.

Grandma nodded and squeezed her hand before heading to the kitchen. From the clatter of pots and pans she guessed that there was still much work to be done down there.

The path I now take
she has taken before,
her sage advice serves to guide me.
Grandmother's wisdom
will point the way
as her spirit walks beside me.

A Moving Promise

Marie shook her head. Forty years in this furniture-packed Victorian! Now she was moving to a small Florida cottage and the idea of packing so overwhelmed her, all she could do was stare at her favorite soap opera and nervously nibble brownies. That's how Jimmy found her.

"Nana," he pleaded, "this stuff has to be packed." The eldest of her six grandchildren, Jimmy was his father's personal emissary. "You have hired a moving company. Haven't you?" No response was forthcoming.

"Want me to start?" he asked.

"Don't worry. It'll get done," Marie grinned, handing him a brownie.

He politely polished it off, then raced home with the news.

"Pop, Nana hasn't done a thing."

"We all tried to help, Son, but she told us to keep our noses out. You know Nana. She'll do it her way."

"Maybe she wants someone to take charge but she's too embarrassed to ask," Jimmy offered as he headed for the phone.

This was somewhat akin to when Jimmy was getting ready to go off to college.

He was the first in the family to go off to school. As the day of his departure approached, the pressure was rapidly building. He wanted to go away to college—and was even looking forward to it. But when it came down to packing all of his stuff into boxes and sealing them with

tape, he froze with trepidation. Nobody had ever moved away from the family before. And he was to leave in a few days. When his parents offered to lend a hand, trepidation turned to frustration.

That was when Nana stepped in.

She swooped into the situation effortlessly—calmly chatting about Jimmy's plans and dreams while casually sorting, stacking, and

packing. Before he knew it, his things were packed and his panic had relaxed.

Now it was Jimmy's turn.

The next day, just as Marie's attack of indecisiveness hit, the doorbell rang. On her porch stood all six of her grandchildren. "Make way for the Delassandro Moving Company," said Lisa, smiling and brushing past her grandmother. Kelly settled Nana onto the couch as Jimmy distributed clipboards. He assigned Kelly and Caroline the kitchen, Dom and Steve the bedrooms, and told Lisa she'd work with him.

"Don't I get a say here?" Marie asked. "I still haven't called a mover."

"Dad took care of that, Nan," Jimmy grinned. "He's got a friend in the business. We have two days to pack you up."

Stunned, Marie proudly watched her moving team meticulously fold, wrap, and box. She particularly loved hearing laughter echoing throughout the rooms as the brigade worked purposefully toward its goal. By day's end, the rooms had been stripped nearly bare.

Promising to return the next day to finish up, six exhausted grand-children filed out the front door as Marie's eyes filled with tears. She was anxious to move, but she would miss each of them—particularly Jimmy, her first-born grandson and the obvious ringleader of this sweet gesture.

Marie opened the door to her bedroom, catching her breath as she switched on the light. The kids had decorated her room with crepe paper streamers, balloons, and curly paper twirls to fill the void of family photos, figurines, and albums that made this place uniquely Nana's domain. Over her bed hung a huge poster, signed by every-one, that read: "We'll miss our Nana, but we promise to visit!"

Just now I can hear my grandmother in my mother's voice, and I think how I will someday sound like my mother. With time, will my daughter sound like me? It is a fascinating legacy, shared impartially among our generations.

Telephone Travelers

Mammaw Maggie threw a farewell party for her daughter, Janet, Janet's husband, and their daughter. But Maggie's heart just wasn't in it.

As she served her guests she listened to her daughter's excited description of her new job, an impressive promotion for one so young. It just happened to be all the way across the country. Maggie was proud of Janet's success that had prompted the move, and she realized with a bittersweet awareness that she had only herself to blame for raising a child so prone to reaching for the stars. But did she have to do it so far away?

They were moving three time zones away. Visiting would become a pilgrimage—a day-long, three-airplane affair. She fretted that Lily, her precious granddaughter, would forget who her Mammaw Maggie was.

The child was equally heartbroken. "I love you, Mammaw," she sobbed the day their overstuffed family car slowly pulled out of the driveway; her sad little face peered out the rear window. Maggie's tear-stained face mirrored the child's.

My days of grandmothering have gone the way of the hand-crank ice cream freezer, Maggie thought to herself as she sat on her front porch steps. She contemplated the forlorn stillness of the swing, and watched the dry, November leaves scuttling across the already fading hopscotch lines on the sidewalk. *I wanted to be an old-fashioned granny like I used to have,* she thought. *A granny who pulled green window shades down, who knew how to make hollyhock dollies and snapdragon puppets for grandbabies living next door. Now I have to make airplane reservations and long-distance telephone calls.*

Maggie was down in the dumps for weeks, sulking and shuffling around the house. She settled back into her routines, but the bounce was out of her step. Winter conversations on the phone, strained with politeness, and letters full of gaps only depressed her more.

As the weather warmed, Maggie stared out at the delicate spring bluebells and sighed. Then a homesick phone call from little Lily spurred her into some action.

"Mammaw," the child said, voice quavering, "I miss you too much."

Not so much, but "too much." Too much to enjoy her new home, school, and friends. Too much to see living in a new part of the country as the adventure that it was.

"An adventure for both of us," Maggie said to herself as she hunted down her car keys and purse.

On her impromptu shopping trip, she didn't find what she was looking for until the third store, but there they finally were: two miniature matching tea sets, old-fashioned pink, yellow, and burgundy hollyhocks lacing their way around the delicate cups and pot. Each had a matching sugar bowl and cream pitcher. "One to keep, one to mail to my granddaughter," she told the clerk.

Lily was delighted when her gift arrived. She called Mammaw Maggie to accept her enclosed invitation as soon as she received it. "You are invited to a tea party at 2 P.M., your time," it read in Mammaw's looping scrawl, "next Saturday."

And so, at precisely 2:00 in the afternoon on Saturday, they met for the first time for a brief tea party served from their matching sets.

Lily's mother fixed tea and cut tiny cream cheese and grape jelly sandwiches on the girl's end of the line, while Mammaw Maggie set

herself a lovely tray of cucumber sandwiches and fresh lemon-mint tea on her screened-in porch back home.

Separated by hundreds of miles, the two were learning that, with the simple dialing of a phone number and shared activity, a great distance can become no distance at all. *Grandmothers,* Maggie thought with contentment, *find ways to cope, just as grandmas throughout history always have.*

She and Lily continued to meet for tea throughout the years, taking turns doing the inviting. It is difficult, they agreed, to feel separated when you share sips of fresh-brewed love.

My family tells me I have my grandmother's beautiful blue eyes. It remains to be seen if I can view life with her remarkable insight.

The Outsider

My brother and I called her Granny even though she wasn't really our grandmother. She lived in southern Georgia where the land is flat, Spanish moss swings lazily from trees, and the gnats swarm in black, static clouds during the sluggish summers. Her old house had a tin roof; when it rained, the patter of raindrops could lull anyone into a sound sleep.

In that house, Granny raised seven children by herself; my stepfather was the youngest. I had always felt like an outsider—even in my own home—after my mother married him. I didn't seem to fit in with the rest of the clan.

I remember Granny best during the summer because that's when we usually visited. One summer, I spent a week alone with this hardworking woman.

Every morning, she was up and running before her feet hit the floor. She started with breakfast, cooking eggs and frying up sausage and bacon from her neighbor's farm. My mouth watered for her home-made biscuits. I always poked holes in them to fill with sweet syrup.

After breakfast, Granny washed the dishes in a porcelain pan in the sink, letting them dry on a drain board. Then she'd wash clothes using the old wringer-washer on the back porch. After the clothes came through the wringer, I'd help her hang them outside to dry. "It'll help sanitize them," she'd say.

When her other grandchildren stopped by, and they always did, she'd make time for them. She asked about their summer and listened to their problems. I noticed how special she made them feel, but no matter how hard I tried to feel a part of Granny's family, I still felt left out.

That summer, she took me on a long walk past her large garden to the pond in back. She sat down on a moss-covered rock while I fished. I wasn't a wimp—I baited my own hook—but I could never get the fish off the hook without being finned. Boys were supposed to be brave, but I just couldn't stand being finned. When I reeled in my first fish that day, I left it flipping and flopping on the bank.

"Aren't you going to get it off the hook?" she asked.

"I will, Granny, as soon as it dies."

Granny ignored me. Reaching down and grasping that fish nice and easy, she pulled the hook out. "Next time, you do it," she said, putting the fish in a bucket.

It took a while, but I finally got the hang of taking the fish off the hook. Though I was grateful for her help, I thought she felt obligated to help me. I felt she had to be nice because her son was married to my mom.

When my little sister was born, Granny painstakingly put together a quilt for her baby bed. I remember thinking, *Of course she made a quilt for her. My sister is her own flesh and blood.*

It wasn't until Christmas that I finally realized she didn't make a distinction between any of the grandchildren. That year, she gave all of her grandkids a gift. The girls were each given a super-stuffed red stocking and the boys received their gifts wrapped in bright red Christmas paper tied up with a gold bow. A gold-painted pinecone was taped to each box.

I sat in a corner munching some candy, knowing I wouldn't get as much as her real grandkids. When I opened my box, I found a pair

of underwear, a box of crayons, and a handful of pencils with my name on them—the same gift she gave the other boys. But inside the box was another package—one with a red bow and a package of gummy worms taped to it. I eagerly ripped it open to see a small fishing tackle box with plastic worms and hooks in it. I smiled, thinking of my previous fear of getting finned by a fish, and when I turned to thank Granny, she winked at me. I knew then that I was, and always had been, a part of her family.

The soft smell of lilac powder, the rich gold of an aging bracelet, the perfect bow made by her rich red lipstick: These simple effects remind me of my grandmother, a woman who did not throw on clothes every morning but rather dressed for each day.

Seeds of the Heart

$\mathcal{I}$ was a city girl raised in the suburbs of Atlanta—except for the year I spent in the country after my mother remarried. I pleaded with her not to remarry, but she wouldn't listen. So I was deep into a foul mood by the time we moved into a clapboard house out in the middle of nowhere that January.

While on the phone with my grandmother, I confided how miserable I was; how I hated the "country bumpkin" my mother had married. My father, a military officer, was the exact opposite of my stepfather. Grandma explained that although he wasn't my father, she knew my stepfather was a good man. "Go ahead," she said, "give him a chance."

The days inched along. In time, the stark winter landscape gave way to lemon-yellow daffodils and pink azaleas. But my heart remained cold toward my stepfather.

At Easter time, Grandma spent a week with us. Early that Friday morning, as I wolfed down my breakfast, I noticed my stepfather turning the soil with a shovel out back. I watched as he broke up dirt clods, tossed rocks, added compost, and raked the soil smooth.

"Let's go out and see what he's doing," prodded Grandma from over my shoulder. We wandered outside for a better view.

Once my stepfather noticed us, he motioned us over. He reached into a brown bag and pulled out a handful of seeds. "Want to help?" he asked, looking from my face to Grandma's. I looked up at Grandma and she gave me a nod and a nudge. We each grabbed a handful of seeds.

Kicking off my sandals, I walked barefoot across the red Georgia clay mixed with topsoil. I loved the coolness of the newly worked earth between my toes. Grandma was right behind me, supporting me like a shadow.

"So what are we planting today?" asked Grandma.

"Those are squash seeds. Later, I'll plant pole beans, cucumbers, and tomatoes," he continued as he raked the soil smooth. Then he squatted, dug his fingers into the soil, and dropped in a couple of seeds. Covering them with dirt, he patted the mound. Grandma and I began to work beside him, and before long we had completed several rows.

Later in the day, I sat at the kitchen table snapping beans with Grandma. "Working with your stepfather wasn't so bad, was it?" she asked.

"I still don't like him," I said stubbornly.

As the summer stretched on in its languid, southern fashion, I found that my fascination with the garden grew with it. Some mornings, as the sun was just blinking over the brightening horizon, I found myself drawn outside to the garden and its new growth. I lifted the leaves of the squash, fingering the golden vegetable's silkiness.

One July day, I picked a large green tomato, feeling the warmth it held from the noonday sun. My stepfather must have seen me, because he stopped picking squash and said, "Let me show you how to fry it."

My knee-jerk reaction inside was, *No thanks!* But I could almost feel Grandma behind me, nudging and saying, "Go ahead."

Reluctantly, I dropped my trepidation and said, "OK." In our small kitchen, my stepfather taught me how to cut a thick slice of the tomato, dip it in an egg mixture, then cover it in cornmeal and fry it in hot vegetable oil. I'll always remember that first delicious bite.

From then on our friendship began to grow.

Grandma had helped me soften the hard-packed ground in my heart. And then my stepfather broke and worked the soil to get it ready for planting seeds. It was soil that had not borne fruit for quite some time, but given the right direction and growing conditions, it eventually yielded life.

Over the years, frying green tomatoes with my children has become a summer ritual. As soon as my grandchildren are older I'll teach them how to do it, once more passing on a bond of love that, I know, will continue for generations. And it never would have begun without a little nudge and a nod from my grandmother.

Grandma made a career of finding that elusive silver lining, and she never missed a day of work her whole life.

Love in Autumn

"*W*hy, the very idea."

"This is not what we want for her."

"And at her age!"

The conversation between my parents and aunts and uncles was high-pitched and outraged. No doubt about it, they were sincerely worried.

As it turns out, they were also completely wrong, which is why my sister, cousins, and I had stopped listening to them. After we got used to the "controversial" idea, it wasn't so bad.

You see, Grandmother Lucy was in love. She and the interim pastor had discovered one another at the church rummage sale. She'd been hanging up a jacket to sell just as he reached for it.

"Our hands touched," she told me later, "and I knew."

The Reverend was freshly retired and had just come to fill in at her church until they found someone permanent.

Between them, they didn't have enough of their original teeth to make a full set, and both boasted replacement parts that creaked when they walked. Combined they had sixteen grandchildren and nine great-grandchildren, and each had been married for a half century to beloved mates now gone. There was that spark, though—so bright it dimmed the youthful ardor of my own so-called summer romances.

We kept a close eye on them as Grandmother Lucy and Reverend Henry sailed serenely through the hypothetical waves our parents were making. They went right ahead making plans for a wedding, honeymoon, and a brief return to town before moving.

Only we grandkids knew that their move was going to be overseas, " . . . the good Lord willing and the creek don't rise," as Grandmother said. She was going to teach while he preached; and in their days off, she confided to me the day we shopped for her wedding dress, they were going to explore their new country. "And one another's hearts," she said with a demure blush.

"No fool like an old fool," was said more times than I could count in the intervening weeks. My parents treated Reverend Henry with the same suspicion and disapproval that they did the guys that hung around my sister and me while both of us were home from college and life-guarding at the local pool.

So it seemed only natural that the grandkids should be the ones to host the engagement party.

At first we thought only a few family members would attend. I'll always believe it was curiosity that got them there. Or maybe it was a chance to find out something new to worry about in Grandmother Lucy's relationship.

We presented Grandmother and Henry with matching fishing hats that we'd covered with patches and symbols from all the places they'd lived and things they'd done. We left the tops of the hats empty. "For your new adventures," our card explained.

They, of course, immediately put them on, causing a few raised eyebrows. Grandmother Lucy's hat perched atop blue-washed hair a few shades lighter than her long dress. She wore the pearls our beloved grandfather had given her. "Something old, something blue, and now something new," she whispered to me, slipping the pearls around my neck when I presented her with the hat.

"Love is where you find it and sometimes, you fear, only where you left it back there in your youth," Reverend Henry observed, holding his wine glass high as he made his toast. "But if, perchance to dream, you rediscover it, love may well be richer and fuller, for true love knows no season for sweethearts. Here's to mine."

There wasn't a dry eye in the place as my parents began the applause. And I have to say, my dad was right about one thing that summer: The young squirts hanging around my sister and me couldn't hold a candle to the Reverend Henry. He'd raised the standard pretty high; true love, even in one's autumn years, knows no season.

When Grandmother speaks, everyone listens. For in her words is a treasure trove of wisdom and life experience from which the entire family can benefit.

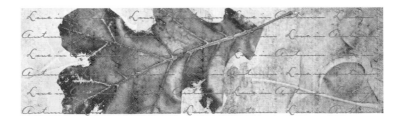

Ladies Who Lunch

"Anyone want to go to Peacock's for lunch?"

Gosh, I loved hearing those words. Every once in a while, on summer Saturday mornings, Grandma would arrive in her sunshine-yellow Cutlass Supreme, walked right into the house without even knocking, and issued her invitation. I would glance down the stairs and there she would be, gray hair beautifully styled, long pink nails perfectly manicured, and impeccable suit embellished with one lapel pin. Her appearance was so regal.

"I do! I do!" I would call down, sending the same gleeful answer every time she invited. I'm not sure why I so looked forward to these luncheons. Peacock's was a sparsely decorated, glorified ice-cream

parlor, but Grandma and I always managed to make a grand afternoon of it.

I would put on my party dress, white lace socks with Mary Janes, and even let Mom stretch my hair into a high half-ponytail. I would always carry a pair of soft, white gloves. I never wore them, and I usually lost one before dessert, but I needed them in order to have lunch with Grandma.

Once at the restaurant, we chose our spot and settled back. I remember the white plastic tables with bright orange or turquoise plastic chairs tucked beneath. I didn't even mind that my thighs stuck to the plastic.

When the waitress arrived, I would order the same cheese-burger, fries, and soda every time, and Grandma would order the same grilled cheese sandwich, without fries, and black coffee. Then, without me even having to clean my plate, she would buy me a big scoop of pink peppermint ice cream.

Throughout the meal, Grandma would ask me about school: Was I getting good grades? She asked about friends: Did I have a boyfriend yet? Or she'd inquire about whatever after-school class Mom had me signed up for. It wasn't particularly memorable conversation.

Grandma and I didn't have that sort of relationship. It was more ladies-who-lunch banter. And that suited me just fine.

After the last lick of ice cream, we thanked our waitress for her wonderful service and, in a very ladylike fashion, Grandma would reapply her lipstick. I knew it was time to leave.

After we returned home, Mom made me change back into my shorts and T-shirt, but I always kept on the pretty white lace socks—just so I could hold on to my lunch with Grandma a little bit longer.

Out of respect for my elders, I listened when Grandma spoke. Decades later, I realize that what I instinctively respected was not age but truth.

My Own Russian Tea Room

When I was a little boy, maybe five or six, my father would pack me in the lime-green Ford Falcon and drive me off to Grandma's house. We did this every third Saturday of every month for several years, until Grandma passed away. After we arrived, Dad would putter around Grandma's house, and I would sip fine, imported tea beside this old, enchanting woman.

Grandma came to the United States when she was 19 years old. She came from Leningrad in the former Soviet Union. Decades later, when I remember Grandma, I always recall the famous words Winston Churchill used to explain the Soviet Union. He described the nation as "a riddle wrapped in a mystery inside an enigma."

I could say the same for Grandma. The riddle for me was why she even bothered coming to America. She spoke so fondly of her childhood home in Leningrad. She would wistfully recall the long, early summer twilights—the white nights. Grandma spoke of the islands forming Leningrad—more than 100 of them—all joined by bridges. She made this Venice of the North sound so romantic, so inviting.

With great nostalgia, she told me about the Dacha, a summer home where her family vacationed. Her family was fortunate, she would tell me, and they enjoyed privileges. As the story goes, her father (my great-grandfather) was a well-respected writer. But he fell out of favor. He began criticizing the government and sent his revolutionary words through the underground. Grandma called it the *samizdat*. I really don't know the end to this story, other than that it brought Grandma and her brother to America.

As I sat beside Grandma, sipping tea and reveling in her halcyon memories, the sounds of Tchaikovsky filled the air. Sometimes, as we listened to the great composer's work, she would read along in her rough English from American storybooks—English versions of ballets such as *Swan Lake, The Nutcracker,* and *Sleeping Beauty.* For my

benefit, Grandma would point to the pictures in the book at the appropriate times in the music. When I looked from the book and up at her face, she would have her eyes closed, silently nodding her head to and fro in time to the music.

Whenever I left Grandma's house, I always felt a little larger. Not taller, but grander—almost magnificent. I realized that I came from a world far beyond my street in my little town. I had a history.

A Grandmother's beauty is timeless and illumined from within. Each line on her face is a celebration of a life made up of moments filled with passion, purpose, and joy.

113

Blonde Like Me

*P*aige cried all the way home from her friend Megan's house, then hurried upstairs to her room so her mother wouldn't see the tears and ask why. She stood before her mirror and stared at the fair-haired, freckle-faced reflection. Her father called Paige his little towhead, a nickname that, for all her eleven years, had made her happy. But now salty tears caught in the corner of her frowning image.

Was she really an orphan like Megan had said? Why did she look so different from the rest of the family? Her mother and older sister had dark brown hair and creamy white complexions. Her father and two brothers were distinctively tall and dark. A new batch of tears trickled over the streaks already on her cheeks. *Foundling,* she thought. She must be a foundling, just like she had read about in that English novel at school last year.

She rummaged through her closet and found a denim sailor-style hat. She plopped it on her head and pulled it down around her ears.

Paige passed days in a melancholy mope. Her mother kept asking what was wrong, repeatedly feeling Paige's forehead with the back of her hand. Paige was beginning to believe that Megan was telling the truth. Then her annual summer week with Grandma came.

Grandma's old farmhouse had been in her family forever, "since Adam was a pup," she liked to say. Grandma didn't miss much, but she didn't pry when Paige continued to be gloomy.

Finally, Paige couldn't stand it any longer. "Grandma, who do I look like?" she blurted. She held her breath, waiting for the answer and watched Grandma's face for signs of some secret lurking there. Grandma just shook her gray head, however, and looked puzzled. "My blonde hair," Paige cried, grasping a clump in her hand.

A knowing look came over Grandma. "Come with me," she beckoned, heading for the stairs. Large, old-fashioned pictures hung in

the hallway. The frames were huge and ornate. Stoic faces looked out from behind them. Grandma pointed to a black-and-white shot of a pretty, fair-haired girl not much older than Paige.

"Who is she?" Paige wondered, almost afraid of the answer.

"That's my picture," Grandma explained, "You're blonde like me. I guess you're a throwback in a household of brunettes."

And her dread lifted just like that. Paige pulled the hat from her head. Not only did she belong, but she was special—the only one who was blonde like Grandma. Wait until Megan heard about this!

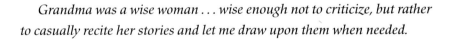

Grandma was a wise woman . . . wise enough not to criticize, but rather to casually recite her stories and let me draw upon them when needed.

Voyager

*S*ean stood six feet four inches tall and was blessed with the looks of a movie star. Add a great sense of humor, a sharp mind, and a heart of gold and you'll understand why he had become valedictorian of Langley High School.

But at the moment, Sean wasn't feeling like a hero—he was paralyzed by fear. He clutched his valedictory speech notes with a tight, sweaty grip that threatened to blur the words before he even had a chance to read them. His name was called, and the audience crackled into applause. He managed (with the help of smiling friends, shaking his hand as he walked) to find his way to the podium.

Sean nervously made a few perfunctory remarks: He thanked everyone for coming and congratulated his fellow "grandmas—I mean

graduates," he stumbled as he and the audience released a low laugh—but it felt good. His pulse slowed. He began his address.

"As your valedictorian, I've been asked to talk about getting the most out of life. I struggled with the topic for weeks. Then I realized: All I have to do is tell you about the person in my life who most knows how life should be lived." The audience grew still as Sean turned a page, then looked up.

"My great-grandmother, Bridget Reilly, was born in a village on the Irish coast in 1898. Orphaned by a plague that was sweeping the nation, she lived with other family members. And although there wasn't much money, she has said that she had a great childhood. She had little schooling, but could read and write. And she had a very adventurous spirit. By the time she was 13 years old, she was working in a bakery to help out with the family's finances."

Sean sipped from a glass of water and gazed out at the audience, now quiet and rapt, held by the years behind this tale. "When Grandma Bridget heard about the sailing of the *Royal Shannon* in 1911, she was fascinated. All over the British Isles, people were being hired to staff the ship, and she managed to talk the shipping line into hiring her as a galley helper. Imagine this little girl—not yet 14 and hardly five feet tall—talking her way onto the ship with only a

single loaf of bread in her hands to prove her baking skills!

"The smooth, expansive seas and the saltwater breeze broadened Bridget's horizons like never before. She liked to stand on deck at night and watch the stars unfold above her. And she had settled into her role as one of many bakers in the ship's galley. Her culinary skills were improving as she learned more about her trade. Bridget's spirits were high, and she felt like her life was just beginning. The world was revealing more of itself to her every day. Little did she know how differently the winds of the world could blow.

"Nobody onboard the *Royal Shannon* could have known that fate had a twist in store for them. Just two weeks into the voyage, a violent storm suddenly struck the vessel. Passengers and crew alike were forced to the interior of the ship as it was tossed and turned in the wild forces of the open ocean. Anxiety onboard was raised a notch as the tempest continued unabated for two days. And then a weakness in the ship's construction was revealed. They were taking on water—not enough to sink, but this storm had cut the cruise short.

"The storm soon subsided, but the *Royal Shannon* had taken a real beating. The captain announced that they would be heading due west to the closest port, on the east cost of Greenland. Repairs were needed on the ship. He said that he was sorry that there would be an early ending to this trip.

"They arrived in Nuuk, Greenland, a few days later. Most passengers, relieved to be off the leaky ship, made plans to head for home. However, most of the ship's humble employees were stranded.

"They were temporarily put up in some drafty storage areas just off the docks. Bridget felt isolated, being marooned in a strange land. But she had decided that she needed to find work.

"The news of the *Royal Shannon's* turmoil at sea soon reached compassionate ears. Donations of food and blankets arrived, as well as a caring American family. The Kellys had emigrated from Ireland to America several years before. They had found prosperity in the New World and were currently visiting family in Greenland. When they heard the plight of this shipwrecked crew, they came down to the docks to see how they could help.

"The Kellys took a particular interest in a young girl who was asking about local jobs in bakeries. She was obviously at her wit's end, but she wasn't ready to give up the fight. They asked this young girl, Bridget Reilly, if she was looking for a way to get back home.

"'Ay. Maybe someday,' she said, 'but I thought that while I'm 'ere, I might as well see what this land 'as for me. Maybe America.'

"Mr. and Mrs. Kelly's hearts instantly went out to this lost, but hardly helpless, little girl. They offered to take her with them on their trip back to America. Grandma Bridget happily accepted, feeling like a star was truly shining just for her. Back in Boston, Massachusetts, the Kellys helped Bridget find a job working in a local bakery. She fell in love with her new land, and decided that it should be her home. She never forgot the kindness of the family who helped her in her time of need and brought her to this wonderful country."

The stillness in the audience was palpable. Sean lifted a hand to his brow to pinpoint his family's location.

"Obviously, all 82 Reillys aren't here today, or none of the rest of you would have seats," he joked. A tension-breaking laugh rippled through the audience. "I think you should meet the woman who best exemplifies some of humanity's most valuable traits, in my opinion." Graduates and guests stirred in their seats as they followed Sean's strides from the podium. His gown billowed around his ankles, and the tassel on his mortar board swung back and forth in front of his grinning face.

Reaching the midpoint of the orchestra floor, Sean extended his hand to a woman so tiny, she couldn't be seen until she stood up. Bridget took a step toward the aisle at Sean's urging, but then he took the kind of action his grandma was known for: He lifted her into his arms and marched down the aisle cradling her securely.

As the audience cheered, valedictorian Sean Reilly carried his 101-year-old grandmother, dressed in her graduation finery, to the stage. Tissues came out of pockets and purses as Bridget's arms tightened around her great-grandson's neck. To Sean's delight, Bridget removed the small pillbox on her head and replaced it with his mortar board. At that point, the few audience members not already on their feet stood to salute the woman who had been one child's hero—but who now claimed the hearts of an entire audience.

I can't wait until I can be a grandmother.

Great-Grandma's Hobby

I'd have to say that my hobby is crocheting. I'm 91 years old and I've probably stitched a piece of clothing for every year of my long life—six afghans already this year. It's such a pleasure planning a project, choosing the colors that go well together, then creating something beautiful out of nothing. It makes me feel like an artist. I try to make each afghan different. I relish the pleasure I see reflected in people's eyes when they receive one of my afghans, as they carefully study the patterns and stitches.

My daughter once asked me how I happened to start crocheting. I thought back to when I was eight years old. It was my grandmother who taught me how.

Growing up, we didn't have much money, so I crocheted edges on towels, handkerchiefs, and pillowcases and gave them as gifts. Later I made doilies, lace collars, sweaters, baby layettes, and toys. My favorite was a cuddly teddy bear I made years ago for my granddaughter when she was just a child.

Time flies just like the stitches I bind. When my granddaughter got married, I presented her with a beautiful peach-colored afghan in a shell pattern.

As I work, I try to keep the stitches straight and even. Crocheting really makes my time worthwhile. When I'm alone, I know that pieces of me are all over the country, snug in the homes of people I love. Just think, I owe all this pleasure to my grandmother, who taught me how to crochet over 83 years ago. Now I'm teaching my great-granddaughter.

Sleepytime Songs

"A tiny turned up nose, two cheeks just like a rose . . . " These words ring like a tender chime in my ears, bringing back the fondest, most loving memories any grandma could have.

My two precious granddaughters, Sara and Laura, heard me sing those words every night as they drifted off to sleep. Although reading was important, and we partook of that activity quite often together, it was my singing the girls required to make their days complete.

I began with the ballads of my youth, songs that I personalized so the girls could make them their own. "I've Been Working on the Railroad" was one of their favorites—Grandpa was a railroad man who worked, "all the live-long day." But "Good Night, Ladies" was the grand finale. If tiny grins appeared on their faces when the first line of that song left my lips, I knew they hadn't had enough and they needed one more song to ensure a restful sleep.

While the songs entered the sweet, cricket-accented, night air, I rubbed each girl's back, soothing away the scrapes and bruises of an active and fun-filled day. I could feel their little muscles relax as I ran my fingers through their hair and sang the notes to "Daddy's Little Girl." They liked that one, too.

The girls are all grown up now—24 and 25 years old. My, how time flies. But those memories, songs, and back rubs will be with me forever—and I hope with them, as well.

Look behind the wrinkles and you will find rich satin.
Explore beneath the pleasantries and you will hear a stream of insight.
Search beyond the end and you will find life.